For Susan, Ben and Eva – and all the rabbits at Marden Hill – C.L.
For Bunny Rabbit, with love X X X – S.A.

Text copyright © 2002 Claire Llewellyn
Illustrations copyright © 2002 Simone Abel
Volume copyright © 2002 Hodder Wayland

Series concept and design: Liz Black
Book design: Jane Hawkins
Editor: Katie Orchard
Science Consultant: Dr Carol Ballard

Published in Great Britain in 2002 as The Best Ears in the World
by Hodder Wayland, an imprint of Hodder Children's Books

This paperback edition published in 2009 by Wayland,
an imprint of Hachette Children's Books,
338 Euston Road, London NW1 3BH
www.hachettelivre.co.uk

The right of Claire Llewellyn to be identified as the author
and the right of Simone Abel to be identified as the
illustrator of this Work has been asserted by them in
accordance with the Copyright, Designs and Patents Act 1988.

Cataloguing in publication data
Llewellyn, Claire
  What's that Noise?: A first look at sound and hearing. – (Little Bees)
  1. Hearing – pictorial works – Juvenile literature 2. Ear – pictorial works –
  Juvenile literature 3. Sound – pictorial works – Juvenile literature
  I. Title
  612.8'5 [J]

  ISBN 978 07502 5878 4

  Printed and bound in China

What's that Noise?

A first look at sound and hearing

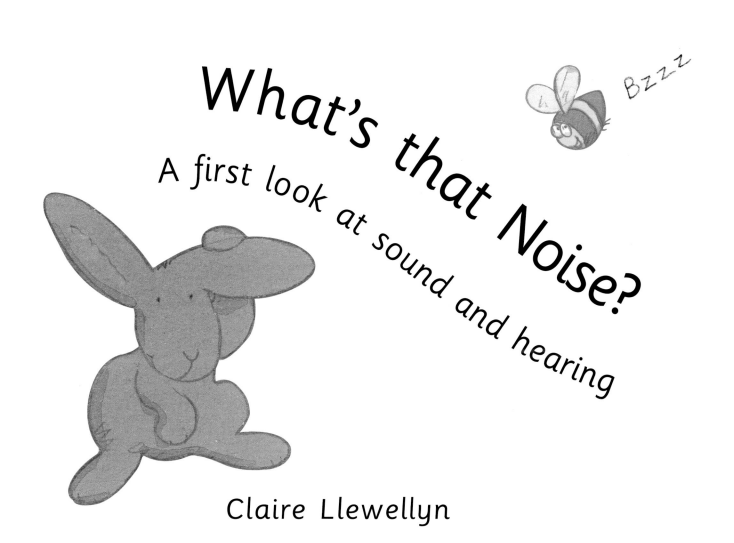

What's that Noise?

A first look at sound and hearing

Claire Llewellyn

WAYLAND

It is early morning. A little rabbit is

Dad, why do rabbits have such silly ears?

looking at himself in the pond.

Our ears aren't silly, son! They're very important.

I think we're going to find out why.

The rabbits make their way along the lane.

They greet the horses in the field.

Suddenly there's an angry gabbling.

The rabbits scamper away.

The rabbits stop to catch their breath,

and listen to a blackbird's song.

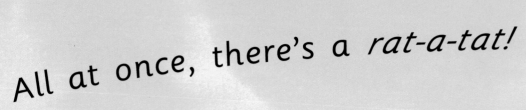

All at once, there's a *rat-a-tat!*

Sounds are made in lots of ways, such as drumming...

Something is coming up the hill.

It's the farmer's noisy tractor.

A moment later the tractor turns

That's better. It's not so noisy now.

and slowly moves away.

There's hardly a sound at the top of the hill.

Sssh! Prick up your ears and really listen.

Everything is quiet and still.

I can hear the buzz of a bumble bee.

You've got very sharp ears!

Bzzz

Now, as the light begins to fade,

the rabbits turn for home.

Suddenly a barn owl swoops.

Eeek!

The rabbits dive for cover.

The rabbits are about to cross a road

when a car roars into view.

They are cosy, safe and warm.

No, Dad. They're not silly. They're the best ears in the world!

29

All about sounds and hearing

Our ears help us to hear.

Our ears tell us where a sound is coming from.

Very loud sounds can hurt our ears.

There are many different ways of making sounds.

Most things move when they make a sound.

Sounds seem louder, the nearer we are to them.

Useful Words

Blowing
Puffing air.

Drumming
Tapping or banging.

Plucking
Pulling an object with your finger.

Wobbling
Moving something to and fro very quickly.

Sounds seem quieter, the further we are from them.